MORGANTOWN PUBLIC LIBRARY
373 SPRUCE STREET
MORGANTOWN, WV 26505

AIR FRYER COOKBOOK

The Top 48 Air Fryer Recipes

TABLE OF CONTENTS

Introduction 1

Chapter 1: The Basics of the Air Fryer 3

    Picking out an air fryer 6

    The Benefits of Using Your Air Fryer 7

Chapter 2: Easy Breakfasts with the Air Fryer 11

Chapter 3: Lunches for Those Days You are Busy 24

Chapter 4: Dinners for the Whole Family 38

Chapter 5: Yummy Desserts to End the Day 53

Conclusion 64

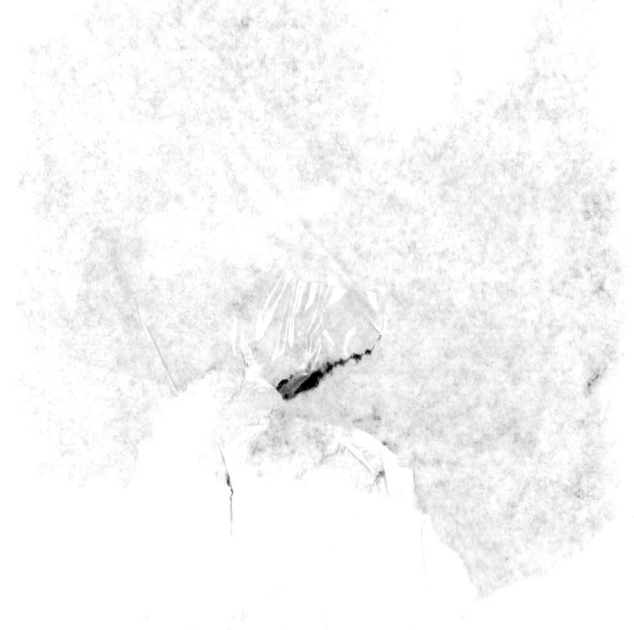

INTRODUCTION

The air fryer is one of the best kitchen appliances that you are able to add into your arsenal. This will make it easier to get a good meal on the table and can even satisfy some of the cravings that you have throughout the day. Rather than wasting all of that money going to a fast food restaurant when you just don't have the time or energy to make your own meals, you will find that the air fryer can meet all of your needs and still provides you with a fantastic meal that you are sure to love.

This guidebook is going to help you to learn more about the air fryer and can even get it all set up for you. You will love how simple it is to use the air fryer, how you have a lot of options when it comes to picking out the type that you want, and all of the benefits will help you to pick out this air fryer as soon as possible.

Once you have a chance to pick out the air fryer that you want to use, it is time to learn some recipes to help you out. This guidebook is going to provide you with a lot of great recipes that will fill you up and work great within the air fryer. We will provide you with recipes that are great for breakfast, lunch, dinner, and even some desserts that are going to help satisfy some of those late night cravings.

When you are ready to stop eating out and you still want to make some delicious meals that satisfy all of your craving even while staying healthy, make sure to check out this guidebook and learn all about the air fryer while also picking out some of your new favorite recipes all in one.

Chapter 1:

THE BASICS OF THE AIR FRYER

There are many people who will worry all the time about getting a good meal on the table. They want to be able to provide for their families, but in between getting to work and school, getting things done at night, worrying about social engagements and activities, and everything else that goes on during the day, it is hard to make sure that you will get a meal that is tasty and nutritious and won't break the bank while being fast.

In addition to always being busy, we all crave some of the foods that are not the best for us at times. We will go through the fast food window or we will pick up something that is in a bag because it tastes fried and good and really can hit the spot on those days that we are just too busy to get it all done on our own.

Of course, we want to feed our family the right things, but when we are dealing with cravings and we are short on time, it can seem like an impossible task. When we are barely making it out the door as it is, it isn't uncommon to spend that time grabbing something out of the freezer or hoping that the drive through window on the way out of town won't take too long to get done.

All of us know that this is bad for our health. Not only is it ruining our waistlines and making it difficult to stay healthy and avoid other issues, it is costing us a lot. Think of the hundreds of dollars that you are throwing down the drain when you choose to go with the fast food or freezer meal options rather than making a meal at home. But, when you have those cravings or you are worried about time, this may seem like the only option.

But there is actually a much better option that you are able to choose from. The air fryer may be the answer to your problems when you want something that is healthy, but will also satisfy the cravings while also sticking with something that will be really fast and won't waste all of your time. There is so much to love about this machine that by the time we are done, you will wonder why you didn't get one of these for yourself years ago.

The air fryer is a simple tool that will use the air and the heat around it to help you to cook up, or fry your foods. You will be able to get the great taste and crunch that you love from some of your favorite restaurants, but since you are using the fraction of the oil, or no oil at all, you will be able to enjoy these foods without all of the guilt that comes with it.

You aren't limited to just some snacks or the regular things that you would think go with your fried foods, you will be able to use this on any of the meals that your family usually enjoys. Later on in this guidebook, we will talk about some of the recipes you can try with it and you may be surprised at what all you are able to do with the whole thing. Most of your favorite meals will work great inside of the air fryer and you are going to be impressed by what all you can make in a short amount of time.

That is another benefit of using the air fryer; it is really quick. Most of the meals won't take that long to cook and you can prepare them ahead of time if you would like. Add them into the air fryer and cook as you get ready in the morning or as you are getting other things ready at night while busy before another thing you need to run off to. Once you put the meal in, you won't have to worry about checking on it too often, except perhaps to shake around the ingredients and make sure that they aren't getting stuck together. Since you are using a bit of heat and mostly air to get this to work, you won't have all the issues that will come up with your regular fryer.

Just look at all of the benefits that you can get when it comes to using the air fryer. You will have the benefits of foods that will deal with those cravings that bother you, the benefit of eating something that is healthier since it doesn't have as much oil in it, and then there is the benefit of how fast you can get some of your favorite meals on the table without all the hassle. Add in all of the money that you will save because you aren't eating out as much, and you will soon want to use the air fryer all of the time.

Picking out an air fryer

When it is time to pick out your air fryer, there are a number of things that you will need to consider to help you make the decision. There are so many great options that come with air fryers that it is likely you will get confused as to which one is the best for you to take home. Some of the things that you should consider when trying to choose your own air fryer include:

- The brand: sometimes you may want to pick out the air fryer based on the brand of it. This will allow you the option to go with a brand that you trust. There are lots of brands of kitchen appliances, but it is likely that your kitchen is full of one over the other. If you have a brand that you really love, it is possible that they have a few options of air fryers that you may want to check out. This can help you to feel more comfortable with the air fryer that you choose.
- The price: the price is something that most people will look at first when picking out their new air fryer. You want to get one that is sturdy and will last a long time, but you also want to get a good deal. You may want to be careful about picking the option that is the cheapest because these often will fall apart or they may cause other issues that you don't want. This doesn't mean that you need to go and pick the one that is the most expensive either. You can look around and compare prices to see which will work the best for you and if you look during certain times, you may even be able to find

some deals on the one that you really want.

- The size: sometimes the size is going to matter so make sure that you are looking at the specs before you pick out your new air fryer. For example, if you are just feeding yourself and one other person, it probably doesn't make sense to pick out an air fryer that is able to feed 10 people because that is just a lot of extra space. On the other hand, if you are going to feed a family, you may want to look for one that is larger to fit in enough food in one batch.
- The review: a good place to look to make sure that you are getting all of the best for the air fryer that you choose is to look at the reviews. There are many reviews that you can look at online for most air fryers and this can give you a good idea of what others thought about this product. Try to read a bunch of the reviews, not just the good ones, so that you have an idea of the good, the bad, and everything in between about the product that you are about to purchase.

Picking out an air fryer will take a bit of time if you want to find one that is amazing for your family. Take your time and look at the options above in order to figure out which one is going to work the best for you.

The Benefits of Using Your Air Fryer

There are so many great benefits that you will be able to receive when you choose to use the air fryer on those busy nights, or on those nights that you are just too tired to make something and want to indulge. You will enjoy that you get to save some money and that you get to enjoy food that tastes unhealthy, but it actually pretty good for you. Some of the great benefits that you can receive when you choose to start cooking your family meals with the air fryer rather than going out include:

- Healthier foods: the air fryer is healthier. Regular frying uses a lot of oil inside of it, which can be bad on many parts of your health. But with the air fryer you are relying on air to heat up the food, which gives the same kind of result but helps to reserve the oil and makes the food healthier. Think of how nice it will be to get all the benefits that you wish without all the bad stuff.
- Satisfies cravings: sometimes we all crave something that is just not that healthy for us. We want that crisp and satisfying taste that we get from fried foods, but we all know that the oils and fat are so bad on the body and can make us feel really sick. But with the air fryer, you are able to get these tastes that you want and all of the cravings taken care of, without having to worry about the unhealthy benefits. You get the good stuff that you want with a fraction of the oil so you can indulge without having to worry. This can make it so much easier to go on a diet or to just take care of your health compared to giving up all that you enjoy.

- Avoid eating out: none of us want to eat out all of the time. Not only can this get really expensive to deal with (fast food meals are ridiculously expensive compared to making a meal at home), but they are also really bad on your health. All of the meals that you will pick out at your favorite restaurant are high in saturated fats, carbs, and calories that will make your heart feel sad, increases your weight, and can even cause diabetes.
- Fast and effective: the air fryer is really fast and effective. If you want to enjoy fried food that doesn't need all of the oil inside and you want to get a meal on the table fast all at the same time, this is the machine to use. You will be able to use just a bit of oil and then place the whole meal into the machine, cook it for a short time (most meals under 30 minutes), and then you can have it on the table and ready for all of your family to enjoy at supper tonight.
- Saves money: one of the main reasons that people will choose to purchase an air fryer is that it will save them a lot of money. Rather than going out to eat all of the time or picking an option in the freezer section of the store that will cost them a lot of money (especially if they do it all of the time), they can make some of their important meals at home in the air fryer. This will end up saving you hundreds of dollars each month when it comes to not having to eat out all the time.

The air fryer is one of the best kitchen appliances that you can add into your home. It will help you to take care of some of those cravings and will ensure that you are giving your family a tasty and delicious meal no matter how busy you may be that day. There are a lot of options when it comes to choosing the right air fryer for your needs and you are going to love all the benefits that you can enjoy. So get ready to pick out the right air fryer for your needs and try out some of the delicious recipes that are inside this guidebook!

Chapter 2:

EASY BREAKFASTS WITH THE AIR FRYER

Morning Time Frittata

Ingredients:

Shallot (1)
Garlic cloves (2)
Mushrooms (4 cups)
Grapeseed oil (2 Tbsp.)
Eggs (6)
Pepper (1/8 tsp.)
Red pepper flakes (1/4 tsp.)
Salt
Dill weed
Cream cheese (1/2 c.)

Directions:

1. To start this recipe, take out a skillet and cook together the grapeseed oil, shallot, garlic, and mushrooms. When these are all done cooking, take them off the heat and let them cool down.

2. Take out the air fryer and turn it on to 330 degrees. Then take out a mixing dish and crack the eggs inside. Beat these eggs with the black pepper, salt, and red pepper.

3. Bring out your baking dish and pour in the egg mixture along

with the mushroom mixture. Top with the dill and then spread out the cream cheese all over the top.

4. Place this baking dish into the basket of the air fryer and place the lid on top. Cook this for about 30 minutes until the eggs have some time to cook through. Serve this warm.

Chocolate Breakfast Treat

Ingredients:

½ c. chopped hazelnuts
1 c. chocolate frosting
1 can biscuit dough
½ tsp. vanilla paste

¼ tsp. cinnamon
1 Tbsp. melted coconut butter
1 Tbsp. water
½ c. chocolate frosting

Directions:

1. Bring out a mixing bowl and combine the chocolate frosting, coconut butter, and water. When this is mixed to be smooth, add in the cinnamon and vanilla paste as well.
2. Bring out the dough and cut it into 8 biscuits, making sure to use your rolling pin in order to flatten out the biscuits. Cut a hole into the middle of each of these biscuits.
3. Turn your air fryer on and let it turn on to 330 degrees. Work in batches and then place the biscuits inside. Cook each of the batches for 10 minutes.
4. When this is done, use the frosting that you made to top the dish and then enjoy.

Bacon Cups

Ingredients:

1 tsp. paprika
¼ tsp. dill weed
½ tsp. pepper
½ tsp. salt
4 Tbsp. buttermilk

4 eggs
4 slices turkey bacon
1 lb. chopped spinach leaves
2 spring onions, chopped
1 Tbsp. oil

Directions:

1. To start this recipe, bring up some ramekins and place some oil on them. Add the onions, spinach, and turkey bacon inside.
2. Bring out a bowl and crack the eggs inside. Mix the buttermilk into the egg mixture and then the seasonings as well. When this is all done, add in this mixture to the ramekins as well.
3. Bring out your air fryer and turn it on to 350 degrees. Place the ramekins inside the preheating air fryer. Let them cook for 20 minutes or until the egg has time to set before taking out and serving with some toast.

Berry Muffins

Ingredients:

Flour (1/3 c.)
Baking powder (1/2 tsp.)
Baking soda (1/2 tsp.)
½ tsp. nutmeg
Anise star (1/4 tsp.)
Cinnamon (1/2 tsp.)
Sugar (3 Tbsp.)
Salt
Cloves
Butter stick (1/2)
Milk (1/3 c.)
Egg (1)
Cherries (1/3 c)

Directions:

1. Bring out the air fryer and let it heat up to 390 degrees. While the air fryer is heating up, bring out a bowl and sift the flour with the baking soda, baking powder, anise star, nutmeg, salt, cloves, cinnamon, and sugar.
2. In a second dish, beat the butter along with the milk and the eggs until they are well combined. Once this is mixed, you can add it into the flour mixture and mix before adding in the cherries.
3. Bring out a muffin tin and place the mixture inside, leaving a bit on the top for it to expand in the heat. Place into the air fryer and then let the muffins bake for about 15 minutes.
4. After this time, take it out of the air fryer and let the muffins cool down for a few minutes before serving.

Raisin French Toast

Ingredients:

Milk (4 Tbsp.)
Cinnamon (1/4 tsp.)
Salt (1/4 tsp.)
Cardamom (1/2 tsp)

Butter (2 Tbsp.)
Raisin bread (4 slices)
Eggs, beaten (2)

Directions:

1. Take out the air fryer and let it heat up to 360 degrees. While you are heating up the air fryer, bring out a small bowl and whisk together the eggs, cinnamon, salt, milk, and cardamom.
2. When this egg is all mixed up, you can bring out the bread slices and let them soak in the mixture on both sides.
3. Place the soaked bread into the air fryer and then cook the bread for about two minutes. After the two minutes, open up the air fryer and turn the bread slices over. Cook for two more minutes at this time.
4. When the French toast is done, take it out of the air fryer and place onto a serving platter. Garnish with some raisins and then enjoy.

Blueberry Rolls

Ingredients:

Bread slices (8)
Ricotta cheese (1/4 c.)
Blueberries (1/4 c.)
Eggs (2)

Evaporated milk (3 Tbsp.)
Sugar (1/3 c)
Nutmeg (1/2 tsp.)
Cinnamon (1/4 tsp.)

Directions:

1. Bring out some bread and take the crusts off. Then lay them on a flat surface and flatten them out with a rolling pin.
2. When the bread slices are done, place a bit of the ricotta cheese on them and then top with some blueberries. Once these are all ready, roll up the bread tightly.
3. Now bring out a small dish and whisk together the eggs and the milk. In a second dish, combine together the nutmeg, sugar, and cinnamon.
4. Dip the bread rolls first into the egg mixture to coat before adding in the sugar mixture. Place them into the basket for the air fryer.
5. Turn on the air fryer to 330 degrees. Let the bread rolls cook inside for about 5 minutes and enjoy.

Oven Baked Omelet

Ingredients:

Eggs (3)
Kale (3 Tbsp.)
Cottage cheese (2 Tbsp.)

Tomatoes (2)
Basil and thyme mixed (1/4 tsp)

Directions:

1. To start this recipe, you can bring out the air fryer and turn it on to 330 degrees. Bring out a baking dish and coat it all over with some cooking spray.
2. Inside this baking dish, place in all of the ingredients and then stir them to combine well. Place that baking dish into the air fryer and place the lid on top.
3. Bake the omelet inside of the air fryer for about 10 minutes or until the egg has time to set. Cool down a bit before serving.

Fruit Roll-Ups

Ingredients:

White bread slices (8)   Eggs (2)
Sour cream (2 Tbsp.)   Cinnamon (1/4 tsp.)
Cream cheese (6 Tbsp.)   Anise star (1/2 tsp.)
Sliced plums (10)   Vanilla paste (1/4 tsp.)
Evaporated milk (3 Tbsp.)   Sugar (1/3 c.)

Directions:

1. For this recipe, bring out a rolling pin and then use it in order to flatten out the 8 slices of bread. Then bring out a bowl and combine together the sour cream and the cream cheese.
2. Place a bit of this cream mixture onto the bread slices. Top with some sliced plums on top of everything else and then roll up these bread rolls nice and tight.
3. Bring out another bowl and whisk together the milk with the egg. In a third bowl, combine all of the ingredients that are left.
4. Take your rolls and dip them inside the egg mixture to coat before rolling it through the sugar mixture. Place these into the air fryer.
5. Turn on the air fryer and let it heat up to 330 degrees. Bake these rolls for five minutes before serving.

Chocolate Donuts

Ingredients:

Chocolate frosting (1/2 c.)
Water (1 Tbsp.)
Cinnamon (1/4 tsp.)
Nutmeg (1/4 tsp)

1 can of biscuit dough
Chocolate frosting (1 c.)
Walnuts (1/2 c.)

Directions:

1. To start this recipe, bring out a bowl and combine the chocolate frosting and the water to make it smooth before adding in the cinnamon and nutmeg.
2. Bring out the biscuit dough and mix it with the chocolate mixture before cutting it into eight parts. Flatten these out as a rolling pin. Make sure to cut out a small hole into all of these biscuits right in the middle.
3. Turn on the air fryer and let it heat up to 330 degrees. Place the donuts into the air fryer and let them bake for about 10 minutes. Depending on the size of your air fryer, you may need to do these in batches.
4. When the donuts are done, allow them to cool down a bit. If you would like, drizzle on a bit more chocolate frosting on the top and drizzle with a few walnuts before serving.

Bacon Muffins

Ingredients:

Oil (2 Tbsp.)
Bacon slices (6)
Corn muffin mix (1 box)
Salt
Pepper
Marjoram (1 tsp.)
Mustard seeds (1/2 tsp.)
Celery seeds (1/4 tsp.)
Scallions (4 Tbsp.)
Mozzarella cheese (1/3 c)

Directions:

1. Take out a skillet and heat up a bit of oil inside. When the skillet is warm, add in the bacon and let it cook for about 6 minutes or until crispy. Once the bacon is done, chop it up and then reserve to the side.
2. Now it is time to make the muffin mixture. Follow the directions on the box to make this muffin mix, but add in the bits of bacon as well as the other ingredients into this batter as well and mix well.
3. Bring out the air fryer and turn it on to 330 degrees. While the air fryer is heating up, take out a muffin pan and pour the batter inside.
4. Place the muffins into the air fryer and let them bake for about 15 minutes, or until cooked through and then serve.

Bread Pudding

Ingredients:

White bread, cubed (8 slices)
Eggs (2)
Milk (1 c)
Buttermilk (1/2 c.)
Half and half (1/2 c.)
Honey (1/3 c.)
Hazelnut (1/4 tsp)
Vanilla (1/2 tsp.)
Butter (4 Tbsp.)
Sugar (3/4 c)
Golden raisins (2 Tbsp.)
Hazelnuts (1/2 c.)

Directions:

1. To start this recipe, bring out a big bowl and place the bread inside. In a second bowl, beat together the rest of the ingredients until they are nice and smooth.
2. Take this second bowl and pour it all over the bread cubes in the bigger bowl. Allow this to set and soak for about 10 minutes.
3. While the bread is soaking, bring out an air fryer and turn it on to 310 degrees. When the bread is done, place it into a baking pan and then inside the air fryer.
4. Bake the bread pudding for about 30 minutes, or until it has time to bake through completely before serving.

Banana Fritters

Ingredients:

Flour (1/2 c)
Cornstarch (2 Tbsp.)
Baking powder (1/2 tsp.)
Baking soda (1/2 tsp.)
Ground oats (1 c.)
Salt
Egg (1)
Buttermilk (1/2 c.)
Sugar (1 Tbsp.)
Cloves (1/4 tsp.)
Cinnamon (1/2 tsp.)
Bananas (2)
Coconut flakes (1/2 c.)

Directions:

1. For this recipe, bring out a big bowl and combine the baking powder, flour, cornstarch, baking soda, salt, and the oats.
2. In a second bowl, whisk together the egg, buttermilk, cinnamon, sugar, and cloves. You will want to make this second mixture into a batter consistency.
3. Mix the second bowl together with the second bowl and then mix it well. Take your bananas and dip them into the batter, making sure to mix it well.
4. Turn on your air fryer and let it heat up to 350 degrees. Place the bananas into the air fryer and let them bake for about 4 minutes.
5. Dust with some coconut and then enjoy!

Chapter 3:

LUNCHES FOR THOSE DAYS YOU ARE BUSY

Stuffed Chicken

Ingredients:

Chicken breast (1)
Cheese (1 c.)
Shallot powder (1 tsp.)
Garlic (1/2 tsp.)
Parsley (1 tsp.)
Egg (1)
Pepper
Salt

Directions:

1. Bring out our chicken breast and use a rolling pin in order to flatten in out. Set this to the side.
2. Take out a bowl and combine together the shallot powder, garlic, cheese, and parsley. Place this mixture inside the chicken and then roll it up nice and tight.
3. Now you will need to take out two more bowls. The first one will hold onto the egg and then the second one can hold onto a mixture of salt, breadcrumbs, and pepper.
4. Place your chicken first into the egg to mix before rolling it

through the breadcrumbs and coating it all over.
5. Bring out the air fryer and let it heat up to 350 degrees. Place the prepared chicken inside and let it bake for about 25 minutes before serving.

Catfish Fillets

Ingredients:

Catfish fillets (2)
Tortilla chips (1/2 c.)
Juice and the rind from 1 lime
Garlic powder (1/2 tsp.)
Parsley (1 Tbsp.)
Salt (1/2 tsp.)
Pepper (1/2 tsp.)
Egg (1)

Directions:

1. For this recipe, bring out the catfish fillets and cut them in half so that you end up with 4 pieces.
2. Take out your food processor and place the tortilla chips, lime, pepper, salt, garlic powder, and parsley inside and let these pulse together for about 30 seconds.
3. Beat the egg and then coat the catfish pieces in it before covering it with the processed mixture that you just completed.
4. Bring out the air fryer and turn it on to 350 degrees. Place the fish inside of the air fryer and let the fillets cook for 15 minutes before serving.

Lunchtime Steaks

Ingredients:

Steaks (2 pieces)
Paprika (1 tsp.)
Salt
Pepper

Canola oil (2 Tbsp.)
Crushed Ritz crackers (10)
Eggs (2)

Directions:

1. Take out the steak and season it with some paprika, salt, and pepper.
2. When this is done, bring out a bowl and combine the canola oil and the crackers inside of one. In a second bowl, place both the eggs and beat them until they start to become frothy.
3. Dip the steaks first into the egg to cover before moving them over to the cracker mixture and covering.
4. Turn on the air fryer and let it heat up to 350 degrees. When this is heated up, place the steaks into the air fryer and let them cook for 10 minutes.
5. Once the steaks are done, slice them into strips and serve with some potatoes or vegetables.

Rosemary Turkey

Ingredients:

White wine (1 c.)
Melted butter (4 Tbsp.)
Turkey thighs (1 lb.)
Garlic cloves (2 minced)
Paprika (1 tsp)
Salt
Pepper
Balsamic vinegar (1 Tbsp.)
Sour cream (1 c.)
Mayo (2 Tbsp.)
Minced rosemary (1 Tbsp.)

Directions:

1. To start this recipe, bring out a mixing bowl and combine the butter, wine, and turkey. When these are well mixed, stir in the balsamic vinegar and the other spices.
2. Place this bowl in the fridge and let the turkey marinate in this mixture for about an hour.
3. When you are ready to cook the meal, take out the air fryer and turn it on to 370 degrees. Place the turkey inside and let it cook for 20 minutes, turning the turkey around halfway through.
4. While the turkey is cooking, start working on the sauce. Bring out a bowl and combine the mayo, sour cream, and rosemary. Serve this sauce with the turkey and enjoy!

Fried Chicken Legs

Ingredients:

½ tsp. salt
1 Tbsp. onion powder
1 Tbsp. baking powder
2 c. flour
1 c. buttermilk

¼ tsp. paprika
¾ tsp. dried dill weed
1 tsp. pepper
1 tsp. salt
2 rinsed chicken legs

Directions:

1. For this recipe, bring out a bowl and place the spices as well as the chicken legs inside. Pour in the buttermilk over the chicken, making sure to get this all around in order to coat.
2. Place this mixture into the fridge and let the chicken marinate inside for six hours or more.
3. In a second bowl, mix together the rest of your ingredients. When the chicken is ready, dredge it through this flour and set aside.
4. Bring out the air fryer and let it heat up to 350 degrees. When the air fryer is warm, place the chicken inside and allow it to cook for 20 minutes.
5. After the cooking time is up, open the lid and turn the chicken pieces over. Cook them for an additional 10 minutes and then serve.

Shrimp Pasta

Ingredients:

Shrimp (1 lb.)
Melted butter (2 Tbsp.)
Dijon mustard (1 Tbsp.)
Chopped onions (1/4 c.)

Garlic cloves (4 minced)
Salt
Pepper
Thyme

Directions:

1. Take out the air fryer and let it heat up to 390 degrees. While that is heating up, bring out a bowl and combine the shrimp, butter, Dijon mustard, onions, garlic cloves, salt, pepper, and thyme. Stir around to make sure that the shrimp gets coated well.
2. Bring out a baking dish and place the shrimp inside. Place the baking dish into the air fryer and let it all bake for about five minutes or until the shrimp is heated up.
3. Serve this with some pasta and enjoy!

Ginger Chicken

Ingredients:

Salt
Pepper
½ c. cream, thickened
½ c. tomato puree
2 minced garlic cloves

1 Tbsp. grated ginger
2 Tbsp. olive oil
2 Tbsp. lemon juice
½ c. Greek yogurt
2 cubed chicken breasts

Directions:

1. Take out a mixing bowl and combine the chicken breasts, Greek yogurt, lemon juice, olive oil, ginger, garlic cloves, tomato puree, cream, pepper, and salt together.
2. Place this into the fridge and let the chicken marinate inside for at least two hours, but going overnight is the best.
3. When you are ready to bake this, bring out the air fryer and let it heat up to 350 degrees. Cook the chicken inside for about 12 minutes and then serve with some rice before enjoying.

Lemon Chicken

Ingredients:

Olive oil (1/4 c.)
Garlic cloves (4 minced)
White wine (1/4 c. dry)
1 lemon juiced
Basil (1 tsp.)

Thyme (1 tsp.)
Salt
Pepper
Sliced chicken breast (4)
Lemon (1)

Directions;

1. Bring out a saucepan and then warm u the oil inside of it. Add in the garlic and let it cook for about a minute. When the garlic is done, add in the white wine and the lemon juice and mix a bit.
2. Now add in the basil, thyme, salt, and pepper and then pour this mixture inside of your baking dish. Add the chicken on top and then tuck in the wedges of lemon all around.
3. Turn on the air fryer and let it heat up to 330 degrees. Bake the chicken for 30 minutes or until it is cooked through before serving.

Beef Schnitzel

Ingredients:

    Beef schnitzel (1)   Olive oil (2 Tbsp.)
    Salt   Breadcrumbs (1/3 c.)
    Pepper   Egg (1)

Directions:

1. For this recipe, take out your schnitzel and then season it with some salt and some pepper.
2. Now take out the first bowl and combine the oil and the breadcrumbs together until they are well combined. Take out a second bowl and beat the egg so that it becomes nice and frothy.
3. When this is ready, dip the schnitzel into the egg to cover and then move it over to the breadcrumb mixture.
4. Take out the air fryer and let it heat up to 350 degrees. Bake the schnitzel inside the air fryer for 12 minutes and then serve with some of your favorite sides.

Beef Alfredo

Ingredients:

Tender beef chopped (9 oz.)   Salt
Chopped scallions (1 c.)   Pepper
Garlic cloves (2)   Dill weed
Sour cream (3/4 c.)

Directions:

1. Take out the baking dish and add in the beef, garlic, and scallions before placing into the air fryer.
2. Allow the air fryer some time to heat up to 390 degrees and then cook the beef mixture for five minutes.
3. Once the meat looks like it is tender, pour the dill, pepper, salt, and sour cream on top.
4. Put the lid back on to the dish and let it cook in the air fryer for another 7 minutes before serving.

Cajun Turkey

Ingredients:

Corn meal (1 c.)
Flour (1 c.)
Cajun seasoning (2 Tbsp.)
Buttermilk (1 ½ c.)
Soy sauce (1 tsp.)
Turkey breast sliced (1)
Salt
Pepper

Directions:

1. You will be able to start this recipe by bringing out three bowls to use. The first one should have a combination of the Cajun seasonings, the corn meal, and ½ cup of the flour inside.
2. Take the second bowl and mix together the buttermilk and the soy sauce until they are well combined. Place the rest of the flour into the third bowl.
3. Take the turkey and season it with the flour first, and then put it in with the buttermilk, before finally taking it through the corn meal mixture.
4. Turn on the air fryer to 350 degrees. When this is heated up, add the turkey breast to the air fryer and let it heat up for 15 minutes. Allow some time to cool before serving with some of your favorite sides.

Stuffed Peppers

Ingredients:

Olive oil (2 Tbsp.)
Garlic cloves (2)
Onion (1)
Ground pork (1/2 c.)
Canned tomatoes (2 c.)
Oregano (1 tsp.)
Basil (1/2 tsp)
Cooked rice (1/2 c.)
Bell peppers (4)
Dry white wine (1/4 c.)
Water (1/4 c.)
Mozzarella cheese (3/4 c.)

Directions:

1. Take out your skillet and add in some oil to heat up. When the oil is ready, add in the onion and the garlic and cook it for a few minutes. After this time, add in the pork and cook long enough for it to brown, making sure to drain off the extra fat that is there.
2. Now you can add in the oregano, basil, tomatoes, and rice and stir it all around. Rinse off your peppers before adding in this new filling and putting the top back on. Arrange inside of your chosen baking dish.
3. Turn on the air fryer and let it heat up to 390 degrees. While the air fryer is heating up, bring out another bowl and whisk together the water and the wine. Pour this in the baking dish all around the peppers before placing it in the air fryer.
4. Cover the air fryer and cook the meal for 10 minutes. Take the lid from the air fryer at this time and cook it for another 10 minutes.
5. Top it all with mozzarella cheese and then serve warm.

Chicken Tortillas

Ingredients:

Chicken legs (4)
Salt
Shallot powder (1/2 tsp.)
Garlic powder (1 tsp.)
Chili powder (3/4 tsp.)
Olive oil (2 Tbsp.)

Shredded cheese (1/3 c.)
Red peppers (1/4 c.)
Lemon juice (1/4 c.)
Chopped scallions (1/4 c.)
Tortillas (12)

Directions:

1. Take your chicken legs and season them with the salt, garlic, shallot powder, and chili powder.
2. Turn on the air fryer and let it heat up to 350 degrees. While the air fryer is heating up, add a bit of oil all over the chicken and then place this into the air fryer basket to cook for 25 minutes.
3. After that time and when the chicken is all done, shred it up and then add it in a big bowl with the rest of the ingredients.
4. Place the corn tortillas onto a flat surface and then top with some of the meat mixture. Serve with a bit of guacamole and then enjoy!

Chapter 4:

DINNERS FOR THE WHOLE FAMILY

Mexican Burgers

Ingredients:

Kidney beans (1 can)
Red bell pepper (1)
Chopped red onions (1/2 c)
Chili powder (1 Tbsp.)
Garlic cloves (2)
Egg (1)

Pepper
Salt
Cumin powder (1 Tbsp.)
Salsa (2 Tbsp.)
Crushed tortilla chips (1/2 c.)

Directions:

1. To start this recipe, bring out a big bowl and empty the beans inside. Take your potato masher and use it to mash up the beans.
2. At this time, add in the rest of the ingredients in the list and mix them together well in order to combine.
3. Shape this mixture into four patties and set to the side. Take out the air fryer and heat it up to 400 degrees.
4. Place the patties into the air fryer and let them bake inside for about 15 minutes or until they are cooked through. When it is

time to serve, place the patties onto a bun and top well before serving.

Pork Ribs

Ingredients:

Rack of pork ribs (1)
Water (1 Tbsp.)
Soy sauce (1 Tbsp.)
Pepper
Salt
Cornstarch (1 Tbsp.)
Vegetable oil (1/2 tsp.)
Five spice powder (1 tsp.)

Directions:

1. Take out the air fryer and turn it on to 390 degrees. Place your ribs into a bowl. Bring out a second bowl and combine the water, soy sauce, pepper, salt, cornstarch, vegetable oil, and five spice powder.
2. When the second bowl is well mixed, toss it in with the ribs and then let these marinate for at least an hour.
3. When you are ready, place the ribs into the air fryer. Let them cook for about 25 minutes before serving.

Spicy Parmesan Chicken

Ingredients:

Breadcrumbs (1 c.)
Parmesan (1/4 c.)
Pepper
Salt
Sour cream (2 Tbsp.)

Mayo (1/2 c.)
Chipotle chili sin adobo sauce (2)
Chicken breasts (2)

Directions:

1. To start this recipe, bring out a bowl and combine the breadcrumbs, cayenne pepper, parmesan, pepper, and salt together.
2. Bring out your food processor and use it to combine the sour cream, chilies, and mayo together until all of your lumps are gone.
3. Coat the chicken with some of the mayo mixture before dipping it into the breadcrumbs and coating all over.
4. Take out the air fryer and turn it on to 350 degrees. Place the chicken inside and let it cook for about 25 minutes. Serve with some sauce and noodles if you prefer and enjoy.

Grilled Halibut

Ingredients:

1 tsp. cumin powder
¼ tsp. pepper
½ tsp. salt
¼ c. lemon juice
¼ c. sugar

½ c. chicken broth
2/3 c. soy sauce
2 minced garlic cloves
2 Tbsp. melted butter
1 lb. halibut steak

Directions:

1. Bring out a skillet and combine the butter, garlic cloves, soy sauce, chicken broth, sugar, lemon juice, salt, pepper, and cumin powder inside. Let this cook up to a boil and then take it off the heat to cool down completely.
2. Bring out a bag and place the halibut steaks and half the marinade inside. Let this set in the fridge for at least 30 minutes.
3. After this time is up, take out the air fryer and let it heat up to 390 degrees. Place the halibut steaks inside and let them cook for 10 minutes.
4. Serve the steaks with some of the extra marinade and enjoy.

Homemade Ravioli

Ingredients:

Eggs (beaten)
Flour (2 c.)
Crumbled Ritz crackers (2 c.)
Cheese ravioli (12)

Directions;

1. You will need three bowls for this one. Place your Ritz crackers inside of one of the bowls, the flour into the second bowl, and then beat the eggs in the third bowl.
2. Take the ravioli and dip them into each of the bowls. Place them first into the egg bowl, and then into the flour mixture, and then into the flour mixture. You can then dip it into the egg and finally through the crackers to finish.
3. Take out the air fryer and let it heat up to 370 degrees. Bake your ravioli inside of the air fryer for 18 minutes, flipping them around at least once during the cooking process.
4. Take the ravioli out of the air fryer and let them cool down a bit before serving with some marinara sauce.

Easy Supper Pizza

Ingredients:

Pizza dough (4 oz.)
Olive oil (1 Tbsp.)
Chopped bell pepper, red (1)
Chopped bell pepper, green (1)
Chopped scallions (1 c.)
Oregano (3/4 tsp)
Crushed basil (1/2 tsp.)
Cayenne pepper (1 tsp.)
Pepper
Salt
Shredded cheese (1/2 c.)

Directions:

1. For this recipe, bring out the pizza dough and add it to a tray that will work inside of your air fryer. You may have to change the size of the dough to make sure that it will fit inside of the air fryer that you have.
2. Take out the air fryer and turn it on to 350 degrees. When the air fryer is heated up, place the dough and the tray inside and bake for 5 minutes.
3. At this time, take the dough out of the air fryer and brush it with a bit of cooking spray. Turn this dough over and bake for an additional five minutes on this side.
4. Turn the air fryer up to 400 degrees, and take the crust out. Take a dish and add in the bell peppers, scallions, and all of the seasonings.
5. Add the vegetables into the air fryer and let them bake inside for five minutes to help them get tender.

6. Spread the finished vegetables all over the prepared pizza crust and top with some cheese. When the pizza is ready, put it back into the air fryer and bake for an additional five minutes.
7. Allow some time to cool down before slicing and serving.

Chicken Nuggets

Ingredients:

Breadcrumbs (1/4 c.)
Cayenne pepper (1/2 tsp.)
Salt
Pepper
Olive oil (1 Tbsp.)

Chicken (1/2 lb.)
Tomato puree (1 Tbsp.)
Eggs (2)
Thyme (1 tsp.)
Marjoram (1 tsp.)

Directions:

1. To get started on this recipe, mix together the breadcrumbs with the seasoning and then add in some oil, mixing around to combine.
2. Take out a second bowl and mix together the chicken breast along with one of your eggs, the tomato puree, the thyme, and the marjoram.
3. Take your second egg and place it into a shallow bowl. Form the chicken into any shape that you want and then coat it in the one egg before dredging it through all of the breadcrumbs.
4. Take out the air fryer and let it heat up to 400 degrees. Add in the chicken nuggets inside and then cook for 10 minutes before you serve.

Country Beef

Ingredients:

Ground beef (1/2 lb.)
Ground pork (1/2 lb.
Worcestershire sauce (1 Tbsp.)
Shallot powder (1/2 tsp.)
Pepper (1/2 tsp.)
Cayenne pepper (1/4 tsp.)
Salt (1/2 tsp.)
Basil (1/2 tsp.)

Directions:

1. To get started on this recipe, take out a bowl and mix together the basil, salt, cayenne pepper, pepper, shallot powder, Worcestershire sauce, ground pork, and ground beef together.
2. When this is well mixed, use our hands in order to form the mixture into four patties.
3. Take out the air fryer and turn it on to 390 degrees. Place the prepared patties into a baking pan and then into the air fryer. Let these cook for 12 minutes until they are done all the way through.
4. When your patties are all done cooking serve them on some hamburger buns along with your favorite toppings and enjoy!

Chicken Meatloaf

Ingredients:

Ground chicken (2 lbs.)
Milk (1 c.)
Tortilla chips mixed with bread crumbs (1 c.)
Eggs (2)
Garlic cloves (4)
Parsley (1/2 c.)
Dijon mustard (1 tsp.)
Salt
Pepper
Cheddar cheese (3/4 lb.)
Tomato ketchup (1/2 c.)

Directions:

1. Take out the air fryer and let it heat up to 390 degrees.
2. While the air fryer is heating up, take out a bowl and mix together the ketchup, cheese, pepper, salt, Dijon mustard, parsley, garlic cloves, eggs, tortilla chips, milk, and ground chicken.
3. When this is done, move it over to a loaf pan and top with a bit of extra ketchup.
4. Place all of this into the air fryer and let it cook for about 45 minutes or until it is cooked all the way through. Serve the mixture warm when you are done.

Beef Chili

Ingredients;

1 tsp. salt
¼ tsp. hot pepper sauce
1 can cannellini beans
1 can diced tomatoes
½ tsp. parsley
½ Tbsp. chili powder
1 tsp. coriander
1 ½ c. vegetable broth

1 lb. beef
½ c. diced green bell pepper
½ c. diced celery
1 chopped onion
2 minced garlic cloves
1 Tbsp. olive oil
¼ tsp. pepper

Directions:

1. Take out the air fryer and let it heat up to 350 degrees. While that is heating up, bring out a pan and mix together the oil with the onion, garlic, celery, and bell pepper. Place these into the air fryer and let it cook for about 5 minutes.
2. After this time, add in your beef and let the ingredients cook for another six minutes. Now it is time to add in the broth, chili powder, coriander, tomatoes, and parsley.
3. Place the lid on the air fryer and let it cook together for an additional 20 minutes.
4. At this time, add in the hot pepper sauce, salt, beans, and pepper. Place the lid on top of the air fryer again and let it all cook together for an additional 10 minutes. Serve this together warm.

Coconut Prawns

Ingredients:

1 beaten egg
2 Tbsp. flour
1 tsp. chili powder
½ c. lemon juice
1 Tbsp. chopped curry leaf

¼ tsp. pepper
1 tsp. salt
½ tsp. garlic paste
1 c. desiccated coconut
4 jumbo prawns

Directions:

1. To start this recipe, take out a large bowl and combine together the garlic paste, salt, pepper, curry leaf, lemon juice, chili powder, flour, and eggs.
2. When this is done, you can dip the prawns into the marinade and then move it over to the coconut and coat it all over.
3. Bring out the air fryer and let it heat up to 350 degrees. When the air fryer is all heated up, place the prawns inside.
4. Cook the prawns for about 8 minutes. When it is done, it is time to serve with some sauce and enjoy.

Spaghetti Bolognaise

Ingredients:

Ground beef (3/4 lb.)
Bell pepper (1)
Celery stalk (1)
Chopped tomatoes (1 can)
Garlic cloves (2)
Pepper
Salt
Cayenne pepper
Spaghetti (1 box)

Directions:

1. Bring out the air fryer and let it heat up to 390 degrees. Place the beef into a baking dish when the air fryer is warm and then add in the beef to let it cook for 12 minutes.
2. After the beef is done cooking, stir in all of your other ingredients, except for the pasta, and then let this all cook for another 18 minutes.
3. While the other ingredients are cooking, you can cook up the pasta in some boiling water until it is al dente.
4. When you are ready to serve, lay the pasta into a platter and then top with your sauce. Mix a bit before serving.

Egg Rolls

Ingredients:

8 egg roll skins
½ lb. shredded pepper jack cheese
Pepper
Salt
1 tsp. cayenne pepper

6 oz. sliced roast beef
2 chopped bell peppers
1 chopped onion
2 minced garlic cloves
1 Tbsp. canola oil

Directions:

1. To start this recipe, take out a new skillet and heat it up with some oil. Add in the garlic, peppers, and onion and cook these for about six minutes before taking them off the heat.
2. Add in the beef to the skillet and then let it cook until it isn't pink any longer. Add in the cheese, salt, pepper, and cayenne pepper. Place the peppers back in as well and mix it well together.
3. Lay out your egg rolls and then place the pepper and meat mixture right in the middle. Roll these up and then use some beaten egg on the edges to help out.
4. Take out the air fryer and let it heat up to 350 degrees. Place your egg rolls inside and cook these for about 10 minutes.
5. After this time, increase the temperature on the air fryer to 400 degrees. Cook the rolls for an additional 2 minutes and then serve.

Chapter 5:

YUMMY DESSERTS TO END THE DAY

Apple Rolls

Egg roll wrappers (16)
Apple pie filling (1 can)
Chopped walnuts (1/2 c.)
Powdered sugar (1/2 c.)

Vanilla (1/2 tsp.)
Cinnamon (1/2 tsp.)
Cloves (1/4 tsp.)
Melted butter (4 Tbsp.)

Directions:

1. To begin this recipe, lay the wraps onto the counter and then divide up your pie filling and the walnuts into the middle of all the wraps.

2. Fold up the egg wrappers like they are burritos and then brush on a little bit of oil before placing them inside of your air fryer.

3. Place the lid onto the air fryer and let it heat up to 350 degrees. You can work in batches on these and then let the wraps bake for about 10 minutes for each batch.

4. While the wraps are baking, you can bring out a bowl and then

combine together the sugar, cinnamon, vanilla, and cloves.

5. Once your rolls have some time to finish baking, you can brush them over with the melted ghee and then dust a bit of the sugar all over them before serving.

Cheesecake Rolls

Ingredients:

Soft cream cheese (8 oz.)
Powdered sugar (1/2 c.)
Vanilla (1 tsp.)

Egg roll wrappers (16)
Blueberries (4 c.)
Butterscotch chips (1/4 c.)

Directions:

1. Take out a baking sheet and coat it with some cooking spray. Set this to the side. Bring out an additional bowl, whip the cream cheese, vanilla, and sugar together.
2. Divide up this mixture among all of the egg roll wrappers and then add some blueberries on top of it.
3. When the wrappers are all filled up, roll them up and seal up the edges. Bring out the air fryer and let it heat up to 375 degrees.
4. Working in batches, place the wrappers inside of the air fryer and cook each of them for ten minutes, making sure to turn them around halfway through the whole process.
5. During this time, bring out a bowl and microwave your chips for about a minute to help them become soft.
6. When the rolls are all done, you can add the chips on top and then serve them warm.

Chocolate Wontons

Ingredients:

½ c. sugar
1 sliced banana
1 c. chocolate and hazelnut spread

1 beaten egg
16 wonton wrappers

Ingredients:

1. Lay out all of the wrappers and coat the edges of them using some egg. When this is done, divide up the hazelnut spread and the chocolate and spread it out among all of your wrappers.
2. Now you can add in the slices of banana before folding the wrappers all over the filling and then seal up the edges.
3. Place the sugar into a bowl and then spray the wontons with some cooking oil. At this time, dip in the sugar.
4. Turn on your air fryer and then let it heat up to 370 degrees. Place the wontons into the air fryer and let it heat up for 8 minutes, making sure to do batches if it is needed.
5. Allow the wontons some time to cool down and then serve.

Strawberry Pies

Ingredients:

Powdered sugar (1/2 c.)
Cloves (1/4 tsp.)
Cinnamon (1/2 tsp.)
Anise star (1/2 tsp.)
Biscuit dough (1 can)
Strawberry pie filling (1 can)

Directions:

1. To start this recipe, bring out a dish and then combine the sugar, cinnamon, cloves, and anise.
2. Roll out the biscuit dough and then make them into some round circles and then make sure to divide up the pie filling between all of the biscuits.
3. Next, dip each of the biscuits into the sugar and then coat them well. Spray with a bit of oil as well.
4. Turn on your air fryer and let it heat up to 330 degrees. Working in batches and place each one into the air fryer. Let these cook inside for about 10 minutes each batch.
5. Cool the pies down a bit before serving.

Chocolate Alaska

Ingredients:

1 lb. chocolate ice cream
6 dessert shells
¼ c. sugar
¼ tsp. anise star
¼ tsp. orange extract
½ tsp. vanilla
½ tsp. cream of tartar
Salt
4 egg whites

Directions:

1. For this recipe, we will need to make up the meringue. To do this, beat the egg whites to make them nice and foamy. When this is done, add in the salt, vanilla, cream of tartar, orange extract, anise star, and sugar. Beat this to make nice shiny peaks to form.
2. Fill out the shells that you have here with some ice cream and then top it with some of your premade meringue.
3. Turn on your air fryer and let it heat up to 420 degrees. Place this dessert into the air fryer once it is warmed up and let it cook for four minutes and then serve.

Lemon Cake

Ingredients:

Sugar (1 c.)
Flour (1 c.)
Butter (2 sticks)
Eggs (3)
Baking powder (1 tsp.)
Lemon zest (1 Tbsp.)

Glaze

Sugar (1/4 c.)
Milk (2 Tbsp.)
Vanilla (1/2 tsp)
Lemon juice (2 Tbsp.)

Directions:

1. To start this recipe, you will need two baking pans. Take out a bowl and mix together all of your cake ingredients with the help of the hand mixer so that it becomes creamy.
2. When the cake is ready, divide up the batter between your two pans and set aside for a minute.
3. Bring out the air fryer and let it heat up to 350 degrees. Place the cake pans inside, or do in batches if it doesn't fit, and bake them for 15 minutes to make the cake golden.
4. While you are baking the cakes, work on making a glaze. Bring out a bowl and combine the lemon juice, vanilla, milk, and sugar together.
5. When your cakes are done, drizzle on some of this glaze and then serve warm!

Cherry Dessert

Ingredients:

¼ tsp. nutmeg
½ tsp. almond
1 tsp. vanilla
Salt
½ c. sugar

4 eggs
½ c. white flour
1 c. milk
¼ c. heavy cream
2 c. pitted dark cherries

Directions:

1. To start, bring out two small pie pans and place your cherries evenly on the bottom of both of the pans.
2. Bring out a pan and combine the milk and the cream together, allowing them to heat up. Cook these together until small bubbles start to form.
3. Whisk this mixture together with the vanilla, nutmeg, and almonds. When they are all combined, pour the mixture over your cherries in the pan.
4. Turn on the air fryer and let it heat up to 330 degrees. Bake the pies in batches if needed for 20 minutes each to allow the topping to brown a little bit.
5. Dust these with some sugar and then enjoy!

Lava Cake

Ingredients:

Butter (1/3 c.)
Chopped chocolate (1/2 c.)
Sugar (1/4 c.)
Flour (2 Tbsp.)
Eggs (2)

Directions:

1. To start this recipe, bring out some ramekins and then grease them up. Dust with a bit of cocoa powder all around.
2. Take the butter and the chocolate and place into a bowl and inside the microwave. Heat these up slowly until they are smooth and melted.
3. At this time, add in the sugar and the flour and slowly fold in the eggs, mixing it all around until it is smooth.
4. Turn on the air fryer and let it warm up to 330 degrees. While the air fryer is heating up, pour your batter into the ramekins and then over to the air fryer.
5. Bake these lava cakes inside the air fryer for 15 minutes giving the sides time to set. Serve them nice and warm.

Mocha Brownies

Ingredients:

Coffee granules (1 Tbsp.)
Eggs (2)
Flour (1 c.)
Baking powder (1 tsp.)
Baking soda (1/2 tsp.)
Chocolate spread (1 c.)

Directions:

1. For this recipe, take out the air fryer and let it heat up to 330 degrees.
2. While the air fryer is heating up, bring out a baking dish and combine the coffee granules, eggs, flour, baking powder, baking soda, and chocolate spread.
3. Pour this into a baking dish and place into the preheated air fryer. Cook these for ten minutes or until they are done.
4. After your brownies are all done, move them over to a cooling rack so they can cool down a bit before serving.

Apple and Peach Cobbler

Ingredients:

Cored apples (1/2 lb.)
Cored pears (1/2 lb.)
Lemon juice (1 Tbsp.)
Cinnamon (1/2 tsp.)

Sugar (1/2 c.)
Flour (1/2 c.)
Nutmeg (1/4 tsp.)
Butter (1 Tbsp.)

Directions:

1. Take out the air fryer and let it heat up to 330 degrees.
2. While the air fryer is heating up, take the apples and the pears and place them into a baking dish. Drizzle a bit of the lemon juice and the cinnamon all over them.
3. Take out another bowl and combine together the remaining ingredients. Sprinkle this topping all over the fruit.
4. Place the pear and apple into the air fryer and let this cobbler bake inside the machine for another 20 minutes so it has time to turn a golden brown.
5. Allow these some time to cool down before serving.

CONCLUSION

Working with the air fryer is one of the best things that you can do for your daily life. The air fryer can save you a lot of time and will ensure that you are able to get a tasty meal that your whole family will be able to enjoy, without having to worry about missing out on your cravings or wasting money by going out.

We spent some time in this guidebook talking about the benefits of using the air fryer and helping you to get it all set up with the air fryer. Once you understand how to pick out your first air fryer and get it all set up, it is time to move on to the majority of this guidebook and learn how to use the air fryer to make some of your most important meals.

We have provided you with many great air fryer recipes that will help you to eat a good meal at any time of the day. Whether you want to use the air fryer on occasion on those days when you are really having a hard day and need to deal with the cravings or you would like to use it all the time for a great meal, you are sure to find a fantastic recipe inside that will meet all of your cravings. Take some time to look through this guidebook and find out some of your new favorite recipes in no time.

MORGANTOWN PUBLIC LIBRARY
373 SPRUCE STREET
MORGANTOWN, WV 26505